Ancient Africa
for Kids

A Captivating Guide to Ancient African
Civilizations, Empires, and History

Table of Contents

INTRODUCTION

Did you know that historians believe the first people came from Africa? This continent has been essential to the development of the world as we know it. There were many different tribes and civilizations in Africa, and some of these ancient civilizations were so powerful that lots of people traveled to them.

But what were these early African civilizations? How did their people live? The history of ancient Africa is filled with fighting armies, wealthy nations, and amazing buildings. They made beautiful art and followed their religious beliefs devoutly to enjoy the afterlife. Both students and parents will enjoy reading this fun, up-to-date history of the civilizations of ancient Africa.

In this book, you'll learn all about the rise and fall of the great Kingdom of Kerma. Kerma eventually became Kush, which became both a friend and an enemy of ancient Egypt. You'll also learn about the wealthy kingdom of Aksum and Ghana, which wasn't anywhere near the nation of Ghana today.

This book has all the information you need to explore early African history. Get ready to dig in and learn how ancient Africa shaped the world around us today.

Chapter 1: The Kingdom of Kerma

Although it no longer exists today, the **Kingdom of Kerma** was once one of the most powerful civilizations in Africa. It was located in modern-day northern Sudan and southern Egypt. It lasted from 2500 BCE to 1500 BCE. That's one thousand years! The kingdom is named after **Kerma**, which is the main city archaeologists have found so far. Its biggest achievement was conquering a big part of the Upper Kingdom of Egypt. The people of Kerma were known for being fantastic archers.

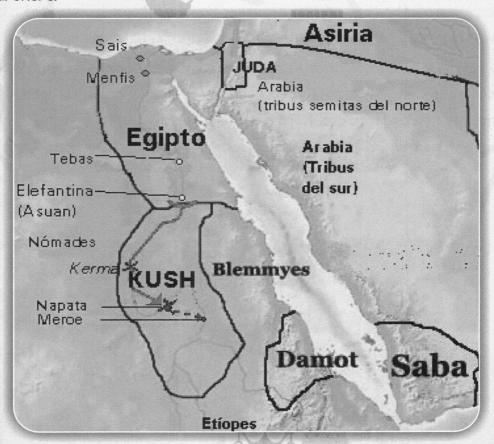

A map showing the location of the Kerma culture along the Nile.

The Kingdom of Kerma didn't just appear out of nowhere, though. Building a civilization like that takes time. Archaeologists believe that people lived along the Nile River in the area as long ago as 5000 BCE. Those first people built villages and trading places. Before long, they were building bigger villages and even cities. They began to conquer more of **Nubia**, which was the area they were in. Eventually, the city of Kerma became the most powerful, and the Kingdom of Kerma took over Nubia in 2500 BCE.

Although the Kingdom of Kerma would eventually be as big as Egypt, its capital would be the heart of its power. For that time in history, the city was big. Many people lived in the city, and it also had a large cemetery.

Archaeologists know that Kerma had a complex social system. While some ancient civilizations had strict divisions between royalty, merchants, and farmers, Kerma seems to have been more diverse. The cemetery reveals that many people had big funeral services. Other

A picture of what the city of Kerma looks like today.

civilizations would reserve such displays for royalty, but Kerma appears to have allowed anyone to have a magnificent funeral as long as they could afford it.

Archaeologists have not found many other cities in the Kingdom of Kerma. However, there were many villages. The farming and fishing villages seem to have been the most important part of Kerma. They sustained the kingdom and helped it become wealthy. The kingdom was split into regions that were ruled by governors called **pestos**. Each pesto had people who reported to him, so the political structure appears to have been complex.

The Kingdom of Kerma lasted for one thousand years. Historians divide the kingdom into three periods. The first period is called **Ancient** or **Early Kerma**, and it lasted from 2500 BCE to 2050 BCE. The second period is called **Middle Kerma**, and it lasted from 2050 BCE to 1750 BCE. The last period is called **Classic Kerma**, and it lasted from 1750 BCE to 1500 BCE.

The Egyptians and the people of Kerma both traded and fought with each other throughout the Ancient Kerma and Middle Kerma periods. They were both powerful enough that their fights didn't really change anything, but their trading helped both civilizations become more prosperous.

All of that changed around 1750 BCE. In 1786 BCE, Egypt was attacked from the north by the **Hyksos** (hik-sôs). They were strong and took over most of the **Lower Kingdom**, which was the northern half of Egypt. Although Kerma was a trading ally with Egypt, the people saw this as a chance to expand the kingdom. They made an alliance with the Hyksos and were allowed to conquer the **Upper Kingdom**, which was the southern half of Egypt. Egypt wasn't completely destroyed, but they were reduced to a small city called Thebes.

The Kingdom of Kerma had its golden age while ruling over the Upper Kingdom. They also took over the Sudanese Kingdom of Sai, so they had a lot of new land and wealth to use. Although they were still very dependent on agriculture, the Classic Kerma period was the height of the kingdom's wealth and power. Everyone who traveled to trade used certain roads and rivers. Kerma had control of the route that went from East Africa to West Africa. They also controlled the route that went between Central Africa and the Mediterranean Sea. They were able to collect a lot of money by charging taxes, similar to our toll roads today.

What ancient Kerma pottery looks like.

The people of Kerma didn't just farm and trade. They also made pottery and metal pieces. They even built monuments called **deffufas** (de-fuf-fa). There were at least three in the Kingdom of Kerma. These were tall structures built from mud bricks that were piled on top of each other to create unique shapes. Archaeologists think they were temples or used for funeral services. The inside walls were usually decorated with tile and beautiful paintings. They were important places for the people.

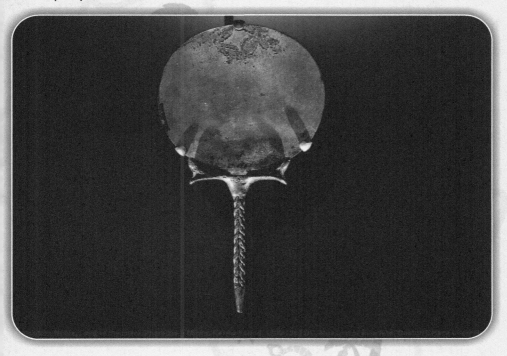

A mirror from the Kerma period.

Sadly, golden ages don't last forever. The people of Kerma had chosen not to move into the Upper Kingdom. Instead, they looted it and then left. The Egyptians who still lived there were loyal to the Egyptian king, not to the Kingdom of Kerma. This was Kerma's big mistake and its downfall.

In 1532 BCE, **Ahmose** (ah-mowz) sat on the throne of Egypt. He was determined to get his whole country back. He was an excellent military leader, and as **pharaoh** (Egypt's ruler), he led the army to defeat the Hyksos in 1530 BCE. Ahmose then turned his attention to Kerma.

Defeating Kerma was a difficult thing to do. They had the usual swords and spears, but their army specialized in **archery**. In ancient times, archers were feared because they could hit enemies at a distance. They could take down their enemy before they could come close enough to fight. The Kermaites were so good at archery that other armies would hire them to train their soldiers.

The Kermaites were also the first people in Africa to use war elephants. You may have heard of other armies using horses in battle, but the people of Africa didn't have horses yet. So, they trained elephants to carry heavy loads and fight in battle. Can you imagine trying to fight against an elephant? It would be really scary!

Ahmose knew that it would be a long fight with the Kingdom of Kerma. There were wins and losses on both sides. Finally, Egypt gained the upper hand under the leadership of **Pharaoh Thutmose I**. Kerma became part of Egypt, and that marked the end of the Kingdom of Kerma. Kerma and Egypt continued to trade and squabble throughout ancient African history because they both remembered being powerful civilizations.

Chapter 1 Activity Challenge

Can you fill in the blanks with the correct keyword?

Sudan and Egypt	Classic Kerma	Hyksos	deffufa
Ancient Kerma	archery	Middle Kerma	Kerma

1. The first capital city of the Kingdom of Kerma was called _____.

2. The kingdom was located in modern-day _____.

3. Kerma teamed up with the _____ to take over Egypt.

4. The _____ period lasted from 2500 BCE to 2050 BCE.

5. The Kermaites built _____ as special temples and for funeral services.

6. The _____ period lasted from 2050 BCE to 1750 BCE.

7. The army of Kerma specialized in _____.

8. The _____ period lasted from 1750 BCE to 1500 BCE and was the golden age of the kingdom.

Chapter 2: The Egyptian Kingdom

Ancient Egypt is one of the longest-lasting ancient civilizations. It existed from 3150 BCE to 30 BCE, when it was conquered by the Romans. But Egypt didn't stop existing under Roman rule. It continued on, and Egypt still exists today as a modern country. Their history is incredibly long and filled with mysterious pyramids, strong pharaohs, and inventions that would change the world.

There were people living in Egypt long before the first pharaoh took the throne. The **Nile** is the longest river in the world, and it flows from the middle of Africa to the **Mediterranean Sea**. This means it flows south to north. Living near the Nile was great for the ancient people. They had a reliable source of water and a way to transport people and goods. They farmed by digging irrigation ditches, and they were protected from invaders by the desert around them.

The people who settled around the Nile lived in two main areas. One group settled near the mountains in the south. They would eventually be called the **Upper Kingdom** because they were upriver. The other group settled down near the Mediterranean Sea. That group was called the **Lower Kingdom** because they were downriver. These two separate kingdoms were always fighting. They had a lot in common, like language and religion, but they didn't seem to like each other very much.

All of that changed when **King Menes I** took the throne in the Upper Kingdom around 3150 BCE. He was also called **King Narmer**. He fought with and conquered the Lower Kingdom, combining both kingdoms into one civilization. This started the **Early Dynastic period** of ancient Egyptian history.

Menes worked hard to convince the people of his new kingdom to get along. He moved the capital to the middle of the country to a city called **Memphis**. He even had a special crown made that had the main color of each kingdom on it to show his people the importance of being united.

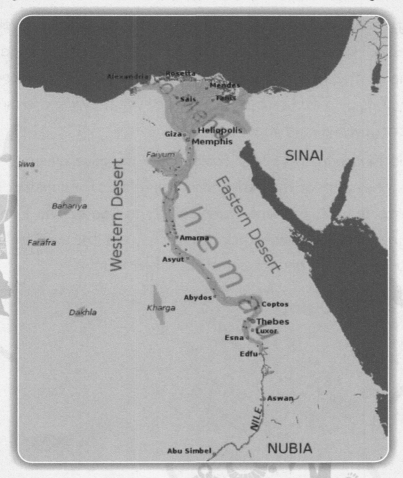

A map of ancient Egypt

The idea of having one ruler over all of Egypt became popular, especially because the people liked Menes. The next period of ancient Egyptian history is called the **Old Kingdom**. The Old Kingdom lasted from 2575

BCE until 2150 BCE. Even though Menes united the Upper and Lower Kingdoms, they didn't have an organized government until **Pharaoh Djoser** (jow-sr) came to the throne. He organized Egypt into **nomes** (districts), which helped solidify the government.

The Egyptians also used **hieroglyphics** to write official government documents. Hieroglyphics was the Egyptians' written language, and it was one of the first in the whole world. Although they were using hieroglyphics by 3100 BCE, Djoser made sure they were writing down important government things.

The Old Kingdom isn't really famous for its government reforms though. The rulers of the Old Kingdom are famous for constructing the **pyramids**. In fact, this time is also called the **Age of the Pyramids**. You might recognize these structures. They are the most well-known structures in Egypt, and you can still see them today!

A picture of the pyramids of Giza.
Walkerssk, CC0, via Wikimedia Commons
https://commons.wikimedia.org/wiki/File:Pyramids_in_Giza_-_Egypt.jpg

The pyramids were built by the pharaohs as special tombs. They were large structures that showed off how wealthy the pharaohs were.

Pyramids were very expensive and very time-consuming to build. Most pharaohs started building their pyramids as soon as they took the throne.

Tombs were important to the Egyptians because they strongly believed in the afterlife. They believed that you had to bury yourself with everything you might need in your next life. They would fill their tombs with treasure and clay figurines. Sadly, other people wanted this treasure too, and most of the treasures that were buried in the pyramids were stolen by 1000 BCE.

But how did the Egyptians build these huge tombs? Archaeologists and historians don't fully know. They think that the pyramids were built by either slaves or local workers. There are ruined villages near the pyramids that show a community was established during the construction. It seems as if houses and food were provided for the workers and their families. Thousands of people had to work for many years to build each pyramid. There are about 138 pyramids in total.

The largest pyramid is called the **Great Pyramid of Giza**. Experts think it took twenty-three years to build and that over twenty thousand people worked on it. That's a lot of people! It took so long because every single stone had to be put in place by hand. The stones were really heavy, and they came from rock quarries along the Nile River. Historians still aren't sure how the ancient Egyptians managed it. Some of these rocks weighed about five thousand pounds. That's two and a half tons!

The ancient Egyptians even managed to build two different types of pyramids. One of the pyramids was flat and sloped on the outside. The other kind was called a **step pyramid**. They had things that looked like stairs on the outside. If the stones were small enough, you could climb all the way to the top.

The Pyramid of Djoser.
Gary Todd from Xinzheng, China, CC0, via Wikimedia Commons
https://commons.wikimedia.org/wiki/File:Saqqara_Step_Pyramid_of_Zoser_(Djoser)_(9794249344).jpg

Inside the pyramids were all kinds of rooms and burial chambers. Once the pharaoh died, he or she was turned into a **mummy**. Mummification was a special process that kept the body from decaying after death. The mummy would be placed in one of the burial rooms with all of the treasures that you could want in the afterlife. There were sometimes even fake burial chambers to confuse robbers.

The ancient Egyptians built many things during the Old Kingdom that we still have today. They built a lot of pyramids, and they also built the **Great Sphinx of Giza**. It has the body of a lion and the face of a man.

The Egyptians built several different sphinx statues to guard places. The most famous one guards the pyramids at Giza.

The Great Sphinx of Giza is the oldest massive structure in Egypt! It was carved out of rock around 2500 BCE. The people in Egypt today work hard to keep the statue in good condition. They have to constantly repair it due to **erosion**, which is the weather trying to break down the statue and turn it into sand.

The Great Sphinx.

Even though the Old Kingdom produced some amazing buildings, it eventually fell. The **nomarchs** (nom-ahrks), or the governors of the nomes, became too powerful. They started to ignore the pharaoh and ran the nomes like private countries. The central government wasn't strong enough to stop them, and it collapsed. Egyptian history moved into the **First Intermittent Period.**

Although the people rallied back together during the **Middle Kingdom,** they were conquered by the Hyksos and the Kermaites during the **Second Intermittent Period**. The Egyptians were left with one major city, so the rightful rulers of Egypt had to huddle together there

The Second Intermittent Period ended when Ahmose I became king. He was about ten years old when he came to the throne, but he would grow up to become a great ruler and military leader. Under his guidance, Egypt pushed the Hyksos out and became a unified country again. This started the **New Kingdom**. It lasted from 1520 BCE to 1075 BCE. The New Kingdom was the golden age of ancient Egyptian history.

During this time, Egypt conquered neighboring nations like Kush, Nubia, and Syria. They also got a lot of wealth from trading and from gold mines. The Egyptians used their new wealth to build temples. One of the most famous temples is the **Temple of Luxor**, which was built in Thebes.

The pharaohs also built special tombs for themselves, but they didn't use pyramids anymore. Instead, they built tombs in a place called the **Valley of the Kings**. Many pharaohs from the New Kingdom are buried here, and archaeologists have found all kinds of important things in these tombs like treasure and mummies.

Although the New Kingdom would eventually fall once Egypt began to interact with Rome, Egypt has remained one of the longest-lasting civilizations in the world. You can still visit it today to see the wonders that the ancient people left behind, which the people today still love and protect.

Chapter 2 Activity Challenge

If you thought this chapter was interesting, there's more to learn about ancient Egypt! Go to your local library or log onto your favorite history website to learn more about the ancient Egyptians. Make sure to always have a parent or guardian helping you with your research. Here are some topics to get you started!

- **Pharaoh Tutankhamun (King Tut)**

- **Moses and the ancient Israelites**

- **Cleopatra**

- **The Library of Alexandria**

- **The sun god Ra**

- **Hatshepsut (a female pharaoh!)**

- **Hieroglyphics**

- **Mummification**

- **Belief in the afterlife**

- **Children in ancient Egypt**

- **Pets in ancient Egypt**

- **The Rosetta Stone**

Chapter 3: The Kingdom of Kush

The **Kingdom of Kush** flowed with riches. Its people specialized in trading iron and gold. Both of those metals were precious in ancient times. Gold is still precious now! But living in a wealthy country didn't mean that things were always great in the kingdom.

A map of the Kingdom of Kush.

The Kingdom of Kush lasted from about 1069 BCE to 350 CE, but there were people in the area long before that. This part of Africa was called **Nubia**. Today, we call it **Sudan**. It is south of Egypt by the base of the Nile River and the base of the mountains. It was a good place to grow crops. Archaeologists believe that people were living in Nubia by 8000 BCE. In fact, the **Kingdom of Kerma** was in the same place! The Kushites shared some of their culture with the Kingdom of Kerma, but they also had things that made them special.

Kush first began to form after Kerma was defeated by the Egyptians around 1500 BCE. **Pharaoh Thutmose III** founded the city of **Napata** to make sure his control over the area was strong. Kush began as an Egyptian colony. It didn't stay a colony forever, though. Napata grew in wealth and power because it had close trade relations with Egypt. The Egyptians also built many temples in Napata, which increased the power of the city. The more temples a city had, the more powerful it was in ancient times.

A model of what the city of Kerma might have looked like. It is likely other large cities, like Napata, looked similar to this.

Eventually, the power of Egypt began to fail after the **New Kingdom** period. The people of Kush took advantage of that and began to exert their independence. Although Kush had existed as an Egyptian territory, the Kingdom of Kush officially began around 1069 BCE. That's when kings ruled Kush as a separate nation without Egypt interfering. Egypt was too busy dealing with its own problems to pay attention to the state just south of them.

The first capital of Kush was Napata. It would be the capital of the kingdom during the height of Kushite power. It was chosen because it had great access to trade routes. Even though Kush was now independent of Egypt, the two still traded with each other. Kush got much of its wealth from trading. Its two biggest resources were gold and iron. Iron was important because it could be used to make weapons. During the Iron Age, whoever had the best weapons tended to win, so everyone wanted the best iron weapons.

Gold was important because it was valuable. In fact, gold was so valuable that the Kushites set up the first **trans-Saharan trade route**. This trade route went over the **Sahara Desert**, which is the biggest desert in the world. Crossing the hot, sandy desert was really hard. It was dangerous because there wasn't a lot of food or water. But as long as the traders had their trusty camels, they could do it. The Kushites built their trade network all the way to West Africa.

The Kingdom of Kush grew richer and richer from trading. Eventually, it was so rich and powerful that it decided it would be easier to just take over Egypt than to continue to trade with them. So, around 746 BCE, **Kashta** declared himself king of Upper and Lower Egypt. He was already the king of Kush, but the Egyptians were so busy fighting each other that nobody challenged him.

In general, the royal Kushites loved Egyptian culture. In fact, the Kushites loved Egyptian culture so much that some historians believe the nobles thought they *were* Egyptians! The Kushites modeled their burial practices, religion, and government on Egypt. They built smaller pyramids as graves. They mummified their dead. They even worshiped the Egyptian gods, although they added a couple of their own gods to the group, like the three-headed lion god. While Kush ruled over Egypt, it continued to support the Egyptian culture. The Kushites even rebuilt some of the important Egyptian buildings.

The Kushites really loved Egypt, but they had some special things about them too. They were known as the **Land of the Bow**. They were really good archers, which was important in ancient times. Archers were range fighters. This means that they could attack an enemy before the enemy could attack them. Archers were important for winning battles.

Of course, the Kushites also had swords and the other usual weapons of war. They were reasonably good at fighting, and they put down several Egyptian rebellions during their rule of Egypt.

A picture of bronze swords from the Kingdom of Kush.

The Kushites did well in Egypt, but their time there was very short. **Shebitku** (sh-bit-ku) ruled from 707 to 690 BCE. That was during the time of the **Assyrians**. They were a powerful Mesopotamian civilization that was conquering pretty much everybody. It seemed as if no one stood a chance against the Assyrians. Shebitku tried to help some of the nations to the north of him fight the Assyrians. Once the Assyrians found out, they were angry. They came to Egypt and defeated the Kushites in 671 BCE. Luckily, **King Taharqa** (ta-har-ca) managed to escape to Napata. The Kushites continued to resist the Assyrians until they were completely defeated in 666 BCE.

This wasn't the end of the Kushites, though. They survived for over one thousand more years after the Assyrians conquered Egypt. They even built another great city called **Meroe** (mer-oh-ee). By about 590 BCE, Kush was getting tired of the Assyrian invasions. They moved their capital south to get away from them, and Meroe became the new capital of Kush.

The Kushites kept following Egyptian practices until **King Arkamani I**, who ruled from 295 to 275 BCE. He is also known as **Ergamenes** (erg-ah-means). He didn't like some of the Egyptian practices. He especially didn't like that the **priests of Amun** were so powerful that they decided when it was time for a king to die. As a new king, that could be scary! Arkamani killed all the priests and made the Kushite people abandon the Egyptian culture. They had to develop their own writing system as a result.

Part of the new culture was women leadership. After Arkamani I, women could be the rulers of Kush. Women were very important to the Kushite culture. The queens did not have to rely on men to give their titles any power. Instead, queens led the Kushite army into battle. **Queen Amanirenas** (a-mon-ur-renas) successfully fought off the Romans and negotiated a peace treaty between Kush and **Augustus Caesar.**

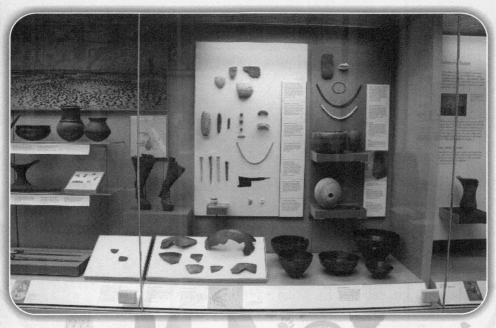

Some of the unique artifacts left behind by the Kushites.
Gary Todd from Xinzheng, China, CC0, via Wikimedia Commons
https://commons.wikimedia.org/wiki/File:Artifacts_from_Kingdom_of_Kush_(35808395143).jpg

The Kushites were a strong people who were good at war and trade. They loved Egyptian culture, but eventually, they developed their own. Kingdoms don't last forever, though. Kush was finally defeated by the **Kingdom of Aksum**. Meroe was in decline at this point. The people were running out of trees to burn for their ironwork, and their farming fields were not producing well. Aksum sacked Meroe around 330 CE. By 350 CE, Kush was another memory in the pages of history.

Chapter 3 Activity Challenge

Decide if the following statements about the Kingdom of Kush are true or false.

1. The Kingdom of Kush began around 1069 BCE.

2. Kerma, Napata, and Meroe were important Egyptian cities.

3. Kush did not have any queens.

4. Pharaoh Thutmose III founded Napata after Egypt defeated Kush around 1500 BCE.

5. Kush was famous for its silver and rubies.

6. Kush was also known as the Land of the Bow because the people were great archers.

7. The Assyrians defeated Kush and made them leave Egypt.

8. The trans-Saharan trade route was first set up by the Egyptians.

Chapter 4: Ancient Carthage

One of the greatest powers of the Mediterranean Sea came from the coast of Africa. We know that Egypt was a powerful country, but they didn't conquer the Mediterranean Sea like the city of **Carthage**. Carthage sits on the coast of North Africa. It is located in the modern country of Tunisia. Although the city does not exist anymore, you can still visit the ruins and imagine what it would have been like to live in Carthage. During the height of its power, it was stunning and wealthy!

The ruins of the Antonine Baths in Cartage.
Dennis Jarvis; author notes these are free to use; https://flic.kr/p/cXmS4G

But Carthage didn't start out that way. The city was founded in 814 BCE by the **Phoenician** (fuh-nee-shn) **Empire**. According to legend, it was founded by a queen. Her name was **Queen Elissa**, but she is also known as **Dido**. She was fleeing from her brother because he was a **tyrant** (a ruler more interested in power than their subjects' happiness). She landed on the coast of Africa.

The **Berber chieftain** who ruled that part of Africa allowed her to build a small city on a hill. He said he would give her as much land as an ox hide would cover. That's not a lot of land for a city! So, Dido had to get creative. She cut the ox hide up into thin strips. She then lined the strips up so that they completely circled the hill she wanted. The Berber chieftain let her have that hill, and she built Carthage.

The city started out as a small trading port. The Phoenicians used it to restock or repair their ships at first. Carthage won its independence from the Phoenicians in 650 BCE and kept growing. By the 4th century, Carthage was a major trading center and the most powerful city in the Mediterranean. The city controlled lots of lands that weren't directly connected to the city. It controlled most of the coast of Spain, the coast of North Africa, and several islands like Corsica, Sardinia, and Sicily.

Carthage got most of its wealth through trade. The rulers charged **tariffs** (special taxes) on the goods that were traded. Trade was so important to the city that it had a special harbor just for merchant boats. The harbor was huge and beautifully decorated with Greek sculptures. It had 220 docks, which means 220 boats could load or unload at the same time!

Carthage had a lot of merchant boats, but it also had a large **navy**. When you have that many valuable goods sailing around, you need to have boats that protect the merchant boats from pirates. The Carthaginian navy sailed all over the Mediterranean Sea to protect other Carthaginian boats and to keep money flowing into the city.

Of course, Carthage didn't only focus on trade. The people were also really good farmers, and they fought many wars with other cities. They conquered land around the Mediterranean Sea to increase trade, and they fought other cities for power and control of the area. The most famous wars that Carthage was involved in are called the **Punic Wars**. The Punic Wars were fought between Carthage and the **Roman Republic**, and they would eventually cause the end of ancient Carthage.

The **First Punic War** started in 264 BCE because Rome and Carthage fought each other over who got to control the island of **Sicily**. The island was divided into different groups called **factions**, and these groups didn't get along. Rome and Carthage supported a different faction, which led to war.

The First Punic War was fought between Rome's army and Carthage's navy. Rome didn't really have a navy at this point, although it worked on building one. Its first few ships were not successful. They were top-heavy and tended to flip over in the water. When you are trying to fight an enemy ship, you really don't want your boat to suddenly flip over.

The First Punic War lasted for twenty-five years. By 241 BCE, the Carthaginians were tired of fighting, so they asked for peace. The Romans celebrated their victory by taking control of all of Sicily and making Carthage pay a heavy fine.

After the First Punic War, Carthage needed more land to expand its trade. It had lost Sicily to the Romans, so it decided to conquer more land in Spain. Unfortunately, the Roman Republic got angry about this. The Romans also had a few cities in Spain, and when **Hannibal Barca**, the general of the Carthaginian army, attacked one of those cities. Rome declared war. The Second Punic War started in 218 BCE.

The Romans controlled the sea, so Hannibal couldn't sneak back to Carthage. Spain and Italy are separated by the **Alps**, a steep and cold mountain range. Most people thought crossing the Alps was impossible. But Hannibal saw it as an opportunity. He marched his entire army over the Alps to attack Rome from the north. He even marched his thirty-seven war elephants over the mountains! Most of the war elephants did not survive the crossing because it was cold and dangerous. It is thought that only one made it across safely.

Once he was in Italy, Hannibal spent the next seventeen years fighting with the Romans. He didn't have a strong enough army to take the city of Rome, but he still won every major battle in Italy. The Roman army could not defeat Hannibal's unique and ingenious battle strategies. They were scrambling to find a way to stop him.

Finally, after huge losses, Roman General **Scipio Africanus** figured out the best way to get Hannibal out of Italy. He sent the Roman army to Carthage, and Carthage called Hannibal back home to help defend the city. This fight is called the **Battle of Zama**, and Rome eventually won.

The Second Punic War ended in 201 BCE. Carthage suffered because it had lost another war. It had to pay a huge fine to Rome, and it had to shrink its army. It also had to give more land to Rome. While Rome thought this was a good thing, Carthage was upset. It was having a hard time defending itself against other African cities and tribes.

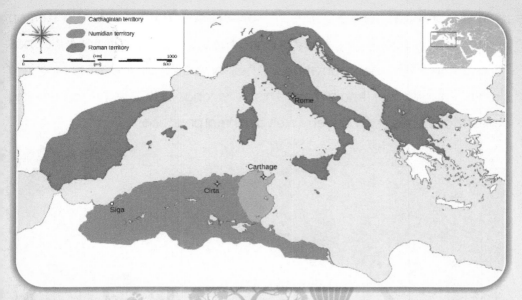

A map showing the three major powers of the western Mediterranean.

By 149 BCE, Rome decided that it wanted to completely destroy Carthage. The Romans didn't like that there was another powerful city on the Mediterranean Sea. They ordered Carthage to dismantle its army and move the city inland. Carthage would be vulnerable to attacks without an army, and moving the city inland would strip away its trading power. Carthage said no.

Rome didn't care that its demands were unreasonable. The Romans declared war on Carthage in 149 BCE and immediately sailed to the city. This war is called the **Third Punic War**. The Romans **besieged** Carthage for three years. Sieging a city is a classic military tactic. An army camps around the city it wants to conquer and makes sure that no one goes in or out. This means that no food or water can go into the city. If the siege is not broken, the city eventually has to surrender so that they can get more food and water.

It took Carthage three years to surrender. When it did, the Roman army destroyed the city. They burned the city down to make sure that no one could live there anymore. They also sold all the survivors into slavery. Today, we know that this is wrong, but back then, selling defeated enemies into slavery was a normal practice.

What Carthage looks like today.
https://commons.wikimedia.org/wiki/File:Tunis_Carthage_Odeon_2.jpg

Carthage was a great African city. It controlled the trade in the Mediterranean Sea for many years, but Rome eventually became more powerful. When Carthage finally fell in 146 BCE, all of its lands became part of the Roman Republic. Rome grew more powerful, building its empire in North Africa on Carthage's foundations.

Can you match the historical events with the correct dates?

201 BCE	146 BCE	264 BCE
218 BCE	814 BCE	650 BCE

1. The year Carthage was first established.

2. The First Punic War started in this year.

3. Carthage was destroyed by the Romans during this year.

4. The year that Carthage won its independence from the Phoenicians.

5. Rome began the Second Punic War with Carthage in this year.

6. The Battle of Zama ended the Second Punic War in this year.

After Rome sacked Carthage, it took over all the land that had belonged to Carthage. That meant that Rome took over part of the African coastline, which is how Roman power first came to Africa. This area of the empire was called **Africa Proconsularis** (pro-kon-su-la-ris), but it is also called **Roman North Africa**. It was focused around where Carthage had been, but it soon expanded westward toward the modern-day Algerian-Tunisian border. It also expanded eastward and southward. In all, Roman North Africa had lands in modern-day Algeria, Tunisia, and Libya.

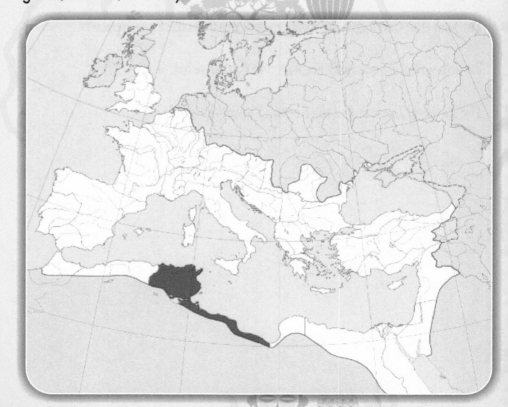

A map of Roman North Africa.

Africa Proconsularis was established in 146 BCE, right after the fall of Carthage. Rome completely destroyed the city, but the land was still good. Some historians believe that when Rome destroyed Carthage, it also sowed salt into the farmland. That might seem strange to us, but if the ground is really salty, plants have a hard time growing. That would make the land bad for farming and keep anyone from trying to live there. Other historians don't think the Romans salted the farmland because as soon as Carthage was destroyed, Rome took over all of that land. The Romans took the best farmland, and they quickly began to grow food. So, it is unlikely that the Romans salted the Carthaginian land, which they used to grow food for their growing empire.

In 122 BCE, **Gaius Sempronius Gracchus** (guy-us sim-pro-ne-us grac-cus) tried to found a colony on the coast of Africa. It was not successful, but many Roman farmers and traders saw an opportunity. They moved to Africa Proconsularis and began working to improve their lives. Rome continued to try to colonize the coast of Africa. By the 1st century BCE, they were successful. **Julius Caesar** started colonizing in 46 BCE, but his plans were finished by **Augustus**.

As the Romans colonized Africa Proconsularis, they had to deal with the **indigenous people** (the people who were already living there). The largest group the Romans dealt with was called the **Berbers**. Historians believe that when the Romans took over the northern coast of Africa, there were several different tribes living there. They had similar customs and traditions, but they weren't the same groups of people. The Romans didn't specify, though. Instead, they called all the indigenous people "Berber," which comes from the Roman word "barbarian." Although we might think "barbarian" is a rude word, the Romans used it to mean anyone who was not Roman.

The Berbers were not strong enough to fight off the Romans, but they were strong enough to survive the Roman invasion. The Roman invasion wasn't the first invasion they had faced. The Berbers had lived in Africa for thousands of years. During ancient times, the different tribes were never able to unite as one group. That meant they were vulnerable to invasions. Other nations set up colonies on their land. All these other people groups influenced the Berbers, changing their culture little by little.

The Berbers didn't keep their own written records, so historians have to trace their history through other records. The ancient Egyptians were the first people to mention the Berbers. They are first mentioned during the Egyptian **Predynastic period**, which lasted from 6000 BCE to 3150 BCE. Both the Greeks and the Romans have records about the Berbers. After Rome fell, the Berber people continued on. They met other groups of people, like the Arabs.

The Berbers are still on the coast of North Africa today. They speak their own language and have their own traditions, like special music and

Berber red slip flagons and vases, 2nd–4th centuries.
AgTigress, CC BY-SA 3.0 https://creativecommons.org/licenses/by-sa/3.0 via Wikimedia Commons
https://commons.wikimedia.org/wiki/File:African_Red_Slip_vessels.JPG

dances. Some Berbers are nomadic and live in tents as they travel with their herds of animals, but most of them are farmers.

The Romans used the Berbers' talent as farmers to help the Roman Empire grow. For a long time, Africa Proconsularis helped produce a lot of food for the Romans. The area was so important that the Romans did a lot of urbanization. **Urbanization** is when people build up a city in a certain area. You might see this happening today. Have you ever noticed a new shopping center where fields used to be? The Romans weren't focused on building malls, though. They were focused on building **temples** and **amphitheaters**.

Temple of August Piety in Dougga, an ancient Roman city in what is now Tunisia.
Dennis Jarvis; author notes these are free to use; https://flic.kr/p/cXfYuJ

The Romans rebuilt Carthage as a Roman city. It eventually became the second most powerful city in the empire. There were also many

estates in the area, which were lands owned by individuals. For several centuries, Roman North Africa did well under Roman rule. It was wealthy. There was a lot of trade. They sold olives, grains, and animal hides. There were also several art schools. There were schools for **sculpting** and schools for **mosaics**. Can you imagine living in such a busy and wealthy area? There would have been so much to learn and do!

The amphitheater in Thysdrus.

Even though the area did well while the Romans lived there, Africa Proconsularis eventually started to fade. By the end of the 300s CE, Africa Proconsularis was not as strong as it used to be. In 430, the **Vandals** reached the coast of Africa. The Vandals were a Germanic tribe. Rome had fought them for years in Europe. As the Roman Empire weakened, the Vandals won more fights. They fought their way into Italy and into Rome itself. It was a huge blow to the Romans. The Vandals began moving all over the Roman Empire, looking for food and money. When they landed on the northern coast of Africa, they made Carthage their new capital.

As the Roman Empire fell apart, the eastern half of the empire grew strong. This empire became known as the **Byzantine Empire**. It had some of the same interests as Rome, but it was not really involved in what was going on in the western half of Europe. The Byzantine Empire did kick the Vandals out of Carthage in 533 CE, but Africa Proconsularis was too weak to defend itself. The mighty Roman Empire was now gone. In 698, Africa Proconsularis gave in to the Arab invaders without much of a fight. Their time as a Roman territory was officially over.

Roman North Africa was an important part of African history. The northern coast was essential to the Roman Empire because it had good farmland. The Romans built cities and let people become Roman citizens. During ancient times, that was a really big deal. For a long time, the area thrived, and you can still visit the ruins today and imagine what living in the second-most important Roman city might have been like.

Chapter 5 Activity Challenge

Can you define or describe the following terms?

1. **Indigenous**

2. **Urbanization**

3. **The Byzantine Empire**

4. **Barbarian**

5. **Africa Proconsularis**

6. **The Vandals**

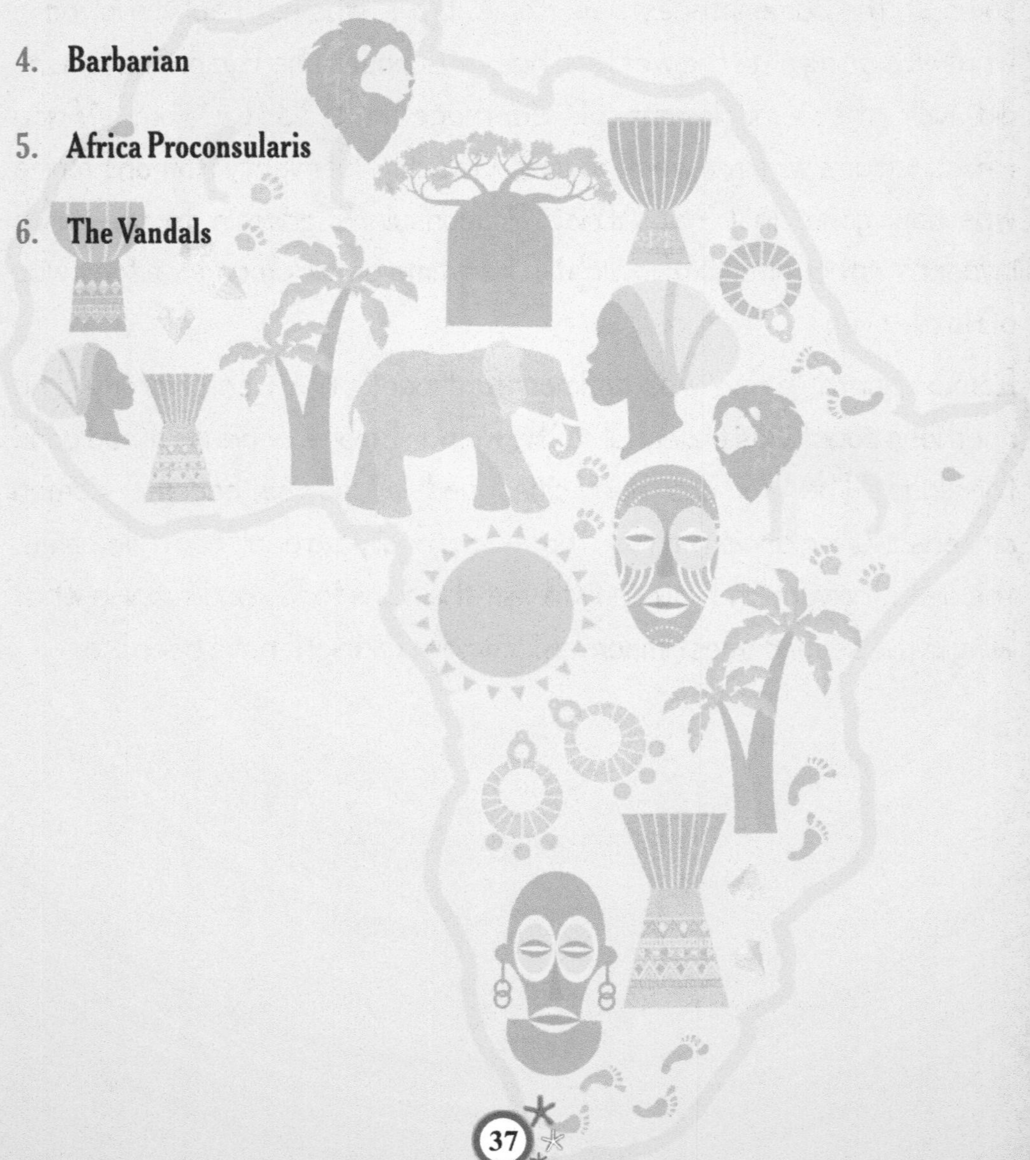

Chapter 6: The Kingdom of Aksum

The **Kingdom of Aksum** was one of the most advanced ancient African civilizations. This kingdom is sometimes called **ancient Ethiopia**. The Kingdom of Aksum had its own coins and written language. During ancient times, this was a really big deal! It shows how advanced they were as a civilization.

Ancient Ethiopia was located on the southern coast of the Red Sea. It covered a big piece of land. The kingdom covered modern-day Ethiopia, Eritrea, Saudi Arabia, and Somalia. The Kingdom of Aksum ruled this area of Africa from about 100 BCE to 960 CE. That's over one thousand years!

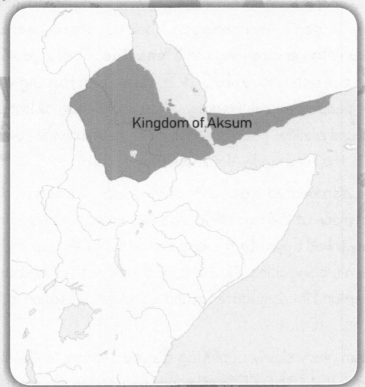

Kingdom of Aksum

A map of the Kingdom of Aksum.

There's a legend that says the Kingdom of Aksum is even older According to legend, the Kingdom of Aksum was founded in 400 BCE by the son of **King Solomon** and the **Queen of Sheba**. King Solomon was a king of ancient Israel, and he was famous for being wise. He was so famous that many other civilizations knew about his wisdom. According to the story told in the Bible, the Queen of Sheba traveled to Israel to talk to Solomon. She was amazed at his wisdom. The Bible story does not mention them having a child. Ancient Ethiopian legend says that they had a son, and he eventually founded the Kingdom of Aksum.

Historians have not been able to prove this story, but they do know that there were people living in that area of Africa long before the Kingdom of Aksum began. Archaeologists believe there were farming communities in this area during the **Stone Age**. The Kingdom of Aksum did not prosper until around 100 BCE. It had rich farming lands, which helped the people become wealthy. They could grow all kinds of grain like wheat and barley. They also had all kinds of animals, like cows and goats. All of this food made Aksum wealthy.

They were also located in a good spot for trade. Trade is all about being in the right place at the right time. And Aksum was certainly in the right place! They linked Egypt to the eastern coast of Africa and Arabia to the western trading cities. All of this wealth gave the Kingdom of Aksum more power, and it consolidated into a cohesive civilization in the late 1 century CE.

The kingdom grew slowly until **King Ezana I** came to the throne. He ruled from 325 to 360 CE, and he was focused on making the Kingdom of Aksum bigger. He wanted his kingdom to conquer more land and become a powerful and important trading center. As the kingdom grew, merchants came from all over the world. They even came from as far away as Rome and the Byzantine Empire to trade at Aksum.

You could find all kinds of things at Aksum. Traders sold gold, salt, precious gems, iron, bronze lamps, olive oil, and wine. Can you imagine what walking through the marketplace would have been like? People spoke Greek to trade, but there still would have been many different languages and so many things to look at. During the height of its power, Aksum was a busy place!

To help make trade easier, Aksum became the first sub-Saharan civilization to make its own coins. It made coins out of gold, silver, and bronze. The coins usually had a picture on them, like a portrait of a king. We know Aksum traded with a lot of different people because their coins have been found in many different countries.

Silver coin of Ezana.
https://commons.wikimedia.org/wiki/File:Ezana.jpg

But the Kingdom of Aksum wasn't only focused on trade. Under King Ezana I, they worked on expanding their land. Aksum conquered the nations and tribes around it, but it didn't rule over them. Instead of replacing their government, the conquered tribes were allowed to rule themselves. They just had to pay **tribute**, which is similar to a tax. They had to pay Aksum hundreds of cattle. We might think that's a weird tax today, but cattle were very valuable back then. In some parts of Africa today, cattle are still very valuable!

King Ezana I fought with the **Kingdom of Kush**. The two kingdoms fought over the ivory trade. **Ivory** comes from elephant tusks, and it is still valuable today. Both kingdoms wanted to control the ivory trade because they wanted to make more money.

Historians are still figuring out who started the war. The written records are not clear. We do know that King Ezana I responded to the conflict by sending a big army to **Meroe**, the capital of Kush. The Kingdom of Aksum destroyed the city and ended the Kingdom of Kush. When Kush fell, Aksum didn't have any other strong enemies. It took control of the whole region.

This made them very wealthy. They spent some of their money on building up their capital. The capital of the Kingdom of Aksum was **Aksum**, but it is sometimes also called **Axum**. To separate the kingdom from the city, we will call the city Axum. Axum started in the 1st century CE, and it's still an active city today. You can visit it in northern Ethiopia. It's a small city now, but Axum is one of the oldest continually occupied cities in Africa.

When Axum was the capital of the Kingdom of Aksum, it was a really important trading center. It also had a lot of ceremonial buildings. The most famous ceremonial structures are the **stelae** (stuh-lay). Stelae were tall towers. Most of them were around seventy-eight feet tall, but the tallest one was about one hundred feet tall. They were usually decorated. They had carvings, stone doors, and fake windows. Most of the stelae were used as tomb markers. They were an important addition to the ceremonial monuments in the capital.

Stelae Park in Axum.
JensiS65, CC BY-SA 3.0 https://creativecommons.org/licenses/by-sa/3.0
via Wikimedia Commons; https://commons.wikimedia.org/wiki/File:Stelenpark_in_Axum_2010.JPG

There were other large buildings in Axum that were probably used by royalty. The large buildings were built with stepped foundations. The

Ruins of Dungur in Aksum.
A.Savin (WikiCommons), FAL, via Wikimedia Commons
https://commons.wikimedia.org/wiki/File:ET_Axum_asv2018-01_img48_Dungur.jpg

rocks were decorated, and there was a special staircase that led to the entrance of the building itself. Some of the buildings had basements and water cisterns inside. For that time in history, having water inside the building was impressive.

The Kingdom of Aksum continued to expand, taking over parts of southern Arabia, which was across the Red Sea. Aksum eventually declined in power. It had to fight rebellions with the tribes it had already conquered. It also had to fight other people who were moving into the area, especially the Islamic people. By the end of the 8th century CE, the Kingdom of Aksum's power was fading, leaving room for another great African civilization to rise.

Chapter 6 Activity Challenge

Can you select the correct answer for these multiple-choice questions?

1. What is another name for the Kingdom of Aksum?

   a) Egypt   b) Ancient Ethiopia

   c) Wagadu   d) Arabia

2. According to legend, who first established Aksum?

   a) The son of King Solomon   b) An Egyptian pharaoh

   c) Hannibal Barca   d) Julius Caesar

3. When did the Kingdom of Aksum first rise to power?

   a) 500 CE   b) 200 BCE

   c) 400 BCE   d) 350 CE

4. What are the tall ceremonial towers in Axum called?

   a) Obelisks   b) Towers

   c) Stelae   d) Guardhouses

5. Which of these places did the Kingdom of Aksum NOT trade with?

   a) Rome   b) Arabia

   c) Great Britain   d) Egypt

Chapter 7: The Empire of Ancient Ghana

The **Empire of Ancient Ghana** (or the Ghana Empire) was another powerful African civilization. It also acquired most of its wealth and power through trade. Ancient Ghana was not in the same place that the **Republic of Ghana** is today. Ancient Ghana was located on the west side of Africa. There were several rivers in the empire, like the **Niger River** and the **Gambia River**. Rivers provided fresh drinking water and food, and they also worked like highways. People would take their boats up and down the rivers with things to trade. Although roads weren't reliable back then, the rivers were. Because ancient Ghana had so many great rivers, it became a very important trading center for Africa.

Map of the Ghana Empire.

Ancient Ghana started in 300 CE, and it lasted until about 1200 CE. We don't know a lot about the early years of ancient Ghana because there is almost no historical information. We do know that the Empire of Ancient Ghana had a king. The king ruled over lots of other smaller tribes. These tribes all had their own leaders, and those leaders all listened to the king. The first king of Ghana was **King Dinga Cisse** (ding-a sis-sa). He came from the **Soninke** (son-ing-cow) **people**, and he brought all the tribes in the area together to form Ghana.

Did you know that this empire had two names? People who didn't live in this area called it Ghana, but the people inside the empire did not. "Ghana" was their word for "king," although it can also be translated as "warrior king." The people who lived in the empire called it **Wagadu** (wa-ja-du).

We don't know much about the early years of Ghana. This isn't a lot of writing from back then. Without written records, historians don't have enough information to get a clear picture of what life was like back then. The first time Ghana was mentioned in writing was during the 700s CE. Ghana had become an important empire by then.

It got most of its power and wealth from trading. Ancient Ghana wanted to get involved with the gold trade because gold was valuable, so it became part of the **trans-Saharan trade route.** They were in the perfect spot for traders to exchange precious items like gold, salt, and iron. Can you believe the ancient people treated salt like it was a valuable thing? We might be surprised because salt is cheap today, but back then, salt was important for survival. Salt helped people preserve food. Your body also needs a certain amount of salt every day. If you don't eat enough salt, you can get really sick. Our food today usually has enough salt, but the ancient people knew how important salt was for their survival.

The people of ancient Ghana didn't only trade with the countries around them. As part of the trans-Saharan trade route, they also traded with the **Middle East**, even though that trip could take forty days. Can you imagine riding a camel across a desert for forty days? That's over a month! Because Ghana traded a lot, it became very wealthy. I charged a tax on everything that came into and left the empire. I goods were coming in, Ghana charged an **import tax**. If goods were leaving, Ghana charged an **export tax**. When you are taxing gold and other precious materials, those taxes can make you wealthy quickly!

The capital of Ghana became a very important trading center. People came from as far as the Middle East to trade in Ghana. The capital

Chinguetti is located in today's Mauritania.

moved a few times during the empire's history. One of the more well-known capitals was **Koumbi Saleh** (com-bi sal-eh). This was the capital during the 11th century CE. Koumbi Saleh was a big city. Archaeologists think that up to twenty thousand people lived in and around Koumbi Saleh.

Ancient Ghana was such a strong trade center because it also had a strong army. It had an army of 200,000 soldiers. The Ghana Empire used its large army to protect its trade routes. Traders were always in danger of robbers in ancient times. Robbers wanted to steal gold and salt, and they weren't afraid to use violence to get what they wanted. Ancient Ghana didn't want to lose its gold, salt, or traders, so it used its big army to protect the traders and their cargo.

Koumbi Saleh, Mauritania.

Ghana also used its army to conquer territories. It took over smaller nations and lands, especially places that produced gold. The richer Ghana became, the more land it conquered. This made it an even more powerful trading empire.

Around 1050 CE, some of the **Muslim** tribes from the north began pressuring Ghana to convert to Islam. They called it a **holy war**. In general, a holy war is when a religious group fights another group or country. They usually say it's about converting people to their religion. Sometimes, it is. Other times, the religious group uses their religion as a disguise to try to get money or power. Many religious groups have fought in holy wars throughout history, and there are almost always multiple reasons for the wars.

The kings of Ghana did not want to fight a holy war. They wanted to continue trading so they could make more money. When they refused to convert to Islam, the Muslim tribes attacked. They didn't hold power over Ghana for long, but their attack weakened the empire's trade. Ghana needed its trade routes to be protected, but it had to spend many years fighting off attacks from these Muslim tribes. All of this fighting made traders feel unsafe traveling to Ghana. Without their trade, the Ghana Empire grew weaker.

Eventually, the lands that Ghana had conquered began to break away. The empire was too weak to stop them. Without land and money, what was left of the great Empire of Ancient Ghana was eventually absorbed by the **Mali Empire**. This ended the influence of this great African trading center.

Chapter 7 Activity Challenge

Can you match the term with the right fact?

1. Wagadu

    a. The most well-known capital of the Ghana Empire.

2. King Dinga Cisse

    b. The king from the Soninke people who united ancient Ghana.

3. Trans-Saharan trade route

    c. The forty-day journey across the Sahara Desert.

4. Gold and salt

    d. The nation that eventually conquered Ghana.

5. Ghana

    e. Literally translates as "Warrior King."

6. Mali Empire

    f. The name that the people used to refer to the empire.

7. Koumbi Saleh

    g. Two very valuable items that ancient Ghana traded.

Chapter 8: Society and Famous Rulers

Ancient Africa was full of advanced societies. The civilizations in this book had class structures and important leaders. They had strong militaries and artists. The civilizations in ancient Africa were important to the ancient world, and they were powerful enough to change world history. Let's look at their societies and learn more about some of their famous rulers.

Egypt

Ancient Egypt was a very wealthy nation. It had social classes, like slaves and the pharaohs, but most people were farmers. They used the Nile to get most of their water because Egypt is really hot and dry. The people didn't get to keep the grain they grew. Instead, it was all stored in royal granaries. Can you imagine how it might feel to put in all the work of growing your own food without even getting to keep it?

The government was mostly ruled by the pharaoh, but the pharaoh had lots of help running the government. There were people like the **vizier** (vi-zeer), who was the chief overseer of Egypt, and the **nomarchs** who were like governors. The ordinary people didn't have any say in their government, but they thought the pharaoh was a god. They didn't have a problem with a god ruling their country.

Pharaoh Menes I

Pharaoh Menes I is legendary. There are historical tablets that have his name on them, but some historians think that "Menes" is a title, not a name. So, some historians don't think Pharaoh Menes I even existed, even though he is supposed to be the first pharaoh of Egypt. They think the first pharaoh of Egypt was named Narmer. Sometimes, the names are used interchangeably.

If Pharoah Menes I existed, he ruled Egypt around 3150 BCE. He is famous for uniting the two halves of Egypt. At the beginning of Egyptian history, the Upper Kingdom and the Lower Kingdom were separate. After Menes became the ruler of the Upper Kingdom, he marched his army up the Nile River to the Lower Kingdom (remember, the Nile flows south to north). Then, Menes conquered the Lower Kingdom and united Egypt into one nation.

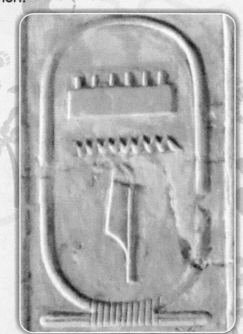

The cartouche (an image of a name) of Menes on the Abydos King List.

Kush

The Kushites loved Egyptian culture, so they modeled their society after Egypt. They had a king and powerful priests who had some say in the government. Most of the people were farmers, and they grew wheat, barley, and cotton. Some people traded things like gold and iron. This brought a lot of wealth to Kush, which allowed them to build things like pyramids.

But Kush also had parts of society that were unique. The Kushites were known for their military. Kush was known as **the Land of the Bow** because it was home to many great archers. Their archers were famous. Good archers were an important part of the ancient military, and Kush made sure that its archers were trained to be helpful during battles. Kush appreciated its archers so much that it even included them in their ancient artwork.

Rulers of Kush.

Pharaoh Piye

Piye (pi) was the king of Kush from around 750 BCE to 719 BCE. He is most famous for conquering Egypt. Kush was located south of Egypt, so it was easy for King Piye to march his army there. Egypt was very weak at this time in history, so it wasn't able to stop Piye. He started by taking over Upper Egypt and conquering the capital of **Memphis**. Then, King Piye marched into Lower Egypt. Many of the Egyptian leaders submitted to his rule, including the last pharaoh of the **23rd Dynasty**. That made Piye the next pharaoh of Egypt. Once he was the ruler of Egypt, Pharaoh Piye returned home to Kush to celebrate his victory. He is remembered in Egyptian history for conquering the nation and helping to start the **25th Dynasty**.

Piye's pyramid at El-Kurru.

Carthage

Carthage was a very powerful empire around the Mediterranean Sea. It got most of its money and power from trade. Only the wealthy and the ruling class could afford to live in houses in the city. The poor people lived outside the city in huts or apartments.

Carthage's government changed during its history. It started as a monarchy. Everyone listened to the king. In the 4th century BCE, the government changed to a republic. Carthage now had a senate that made the laws. The senate was made up of three hundred wealthy men. Carthage also elected two leaders every year called **suffetes** (su-feets) to help lead the empire.

Hannibal Barca

Hannibal was one of the greatest generals in history. He was one of the generals for Carthage during the **Second and Third Punic Wars**. Rome was fighting with Carthage, and Hannibal decided to attack Rome from a direction they didn't expect. Italy has the **Alps** on its northern border. Mountains are a good natural defense system because they are hard to get over. Hannibal didn't let the mountains scare him away. Instead, he marched his army over the Alps and into Italy. He even tried to take his war elephants over the mountains!

Hannibal then spent the next fifteen years in Italy fighting the Romans. He won many battles, even though he had fewer soldiers. This was because he managed to outsmart the Romans. They were scared of what Hannibal might do, but he never took Rome.

Hannibal and the Romans reached a **stalemate**, which is when neither side is really the winner. Hannibal eventually had to go back to Carthage. Ultimately, Rome won the Second Punic War, as well as the Third Punic War.

General Hannibal.
https://commons.wikimedia.org/wiki/File:Mommsen_p265.jpg

Aksum

Aksum got most of its wealth from trade, but it did have a strong military and lots of farmers. Aksum had lots of hills, so the people used **terrace farming** to grow more crops. Terrace farming is when people make large flat surfaces on the side of hills. The flat surfaces look like giant stairs when it's done. It helps people grow more food.

The society of Aksum was very advanced. The people had a written language. They also made their own coins. Instead of just trading and bartering, they used money to pay for things, just like we do. After the 4th century, Christianity became an important part of their society because King Ezana converted to that religion. The people built lots of churches, but it took a couple of centuries for the temples to close down in some of the cities.

King Ezana

King Ezana was the king who helped Aksum defeat **Kush**. He ruled Aksum from about 325 to 360 CE. To help his country grow stronger, he conquered the nearby lands. Kush was close by, and it wasn't the big and powerful country it used to be. King Ezana destroyed its capital, **Meroe**, and took the land for his own kingdom. Aksum was now free to grow and become a strong nation built on trade, and it was all thanks to King Ezana's hard work.

Ancient Ghana

Ancient Ghana was famous for its trade and ironworkers, but most of the people who lived in Ghana were farmers. The local leader gave everyone a piece of land to grow crops on. The farmers didn't even own their land! Despite that, they still lived good lives. The people were safe and had plenty to eat.

The Ghana Empire was a **monarchy**. This means the king was in charge. But the king usually let the local tribal leaders run their tribes. They still had to obey the king, but they also still had some power. When the king died, the next king was his sister's son. This is a little different than other kingdoms, but it certainly worked well for the Ghana Empire.

King Dinga Cisse

Dinga Cisse was the first king of Ghana. Before him, Ghana wasn't really a kingdom at all. Instead, the area was home to several different tribes. Although they sometimes worked together, they were still different groups.

That all changed with Dinga Cisse. He came from the Soninke people, and he united the tribes in the area under one ruler. Because he united the tribes, he was the first ruler. The Soninke people were very important in the government because they were King Dinga Cisse's people.

Chapter 8 Activity Challenge

Can you match the leader with their civilization?

1. **Hannibal Barca**

2. **Pharaoh Piye**

3. **King Dinga Cisse**

4. **Pharaoh Menes I**

5. **King Ezana**

a. **Egypt**

b. **Ancient Ghana**

c. **Carthage**

d. **Kush**

e. **Aksum**

Chapter 9: Culture and Art

The civilizations in ancient Africa were more than just important trading posts. They were important societies that had culture and art.

One of the most important parts of any civilization is its **written language**. In fact, historians say that a written language is essential to a group of people actually being a civilization. Writing is important to understand history. We can learn a lot about people by what they write down. We learn more from what they write down than from the things they leave behind, like tools or houses. But every civilization has its own language, which means they write things down differently.

Ancient Egypt used a writing style called **hieroglyphics**. They used pictures to represent letters or even whole words. You could write your hieroglyphics in any way you wanted to. You could write it upside down or right to left. It makes it a little confusing to translate today. The ancient Egyptians also used **Hieratic** (hahy-uh-rat-ik) and **Demotic** (dih-mot-ik) writing systems. Hieratic was like hieroglyphics, but it was simpler and had fewer symbols. Demotic has no symbols at all, and it looks more like other ancient writing systems.

Kush used a lot of different writing systems, including the same writing systems that the Egyptians used. They also wrote in Old Nubian and in **Meroitic** (meh-row-i-tuhk). Meroitic was invented in the 1st century BCE. **King Arkamani I** wanted to move away from Egyptian culture, so he made the people of Kush get rid of everything Egyptian, including hieroglyphics. Historians aren't able to translate Meroitic, though! They are still working on learning the language. Until then, they don't know what the Kushite documents written in Meroitic say.

Because of the Roman influence, a lot of North African civilizations wrote in Latin. Aksum invented a writing system called **Ge'ez** (gee-ez). It had letters for vowels and consonants, but their letters look very different from letters in the English language. Ge'ez became popular in Aksum as a written language, and it is still used today in Ethiopia.

Did you know that civilizations can use multiple languages? Aksum was such a big trading center in the ancient world that it didn't only use its language. The people wrote a lot of things down in Ge'ez, but they used ancient Greek as a commonly spoken language. It made it easier to trade in the market because everyone could understand each other.

Of course, writing isn't the only part of a culture. **Architecture** is also really important. Architecture is the art of making buildings and monuments. Historians and archaeologists usually focus on really important buildings because they were built for a special reason.

Both ancient Egypt and Kush built pyramids. Ancient Egypt built its pyramids during the **Old Kingdom**, and they were built as burial places for the pharaohs. Some of the Egyptian pyramids have steps, like the **Step Pyramid of Djoser at Saqqara** (suh-kahr-uh). It was built around 2630 BCE. It's over four thousand years old!

Other pyramids in Egypt have smooth sides. The most famous smooth pyramids are the **pyramids of Giza**. There are several pyramids close together in Giza, and they were built out of blocks of limestone. Historians don't know how the Egyptians moved the limestone and stacked it perfectly, but you can still see the pyramids in Egypt today.

The pyramids of Giza.
Ricardo Liberato, CC BY-SA 2.0 https://creativecommons.org/licenses/by-sa/2.0
via Wikimedia Commons; https://commons.wikimedia.org/wiki/File:All_Gizah_Pyramids.jpg

Ancient Egypt wasn't the only civilization to build pyramids. The Kushites
loved Egyptian culture so much that they also built pyramids. They used

Nubian pyramids.
https://commons.wikimedia.org/wiki/File:Nubia_pyramids1.JPG

their pyramids as burial tombs as well. Kushite leaders were ever turned into mummies after they died. Their pyramid would be filled with treasures to help them in the next life. Kushite pyramids were usually smaller than Egyptian pyramids, and you can still see them today.

Unlike Egypt and Kush, Aksum did not build pyramids. They are most famous for tall towers called **stelae**. The tallest stela was about 108 feet tall, but most of them were about 78 feet tall. The stelae were ceremonial. They were usually grave markers, and they were decorated with doors and fake windows.

The people of Aksum also built their stone palaces and other buildings without **mortar**. Mortar is the mixture that holds bricks and stones together like glue. Instead of mortar, the people made sure the stones fit together very tightly. They would decorate their stone buildings with clay.

Dry-laid stone structure in Sukur, Nigeria.
SULE, CC BY-SA 4.0 https://creativecommons.org/licenses/by-sa/4.0
via Wikimedia Commons; https://commons.wikimedia.org/wiki/File:Sukur-8.jpg

After the 4th century CE, Aksum began building churches. Christianity was popular in the kingdom, so they devoted energy to making churches. The old temples were still open into the 6th century CE, so for a while, the two religions coexisted.

The ruins of a temple at Yeha, Ethiopia.

Architecture is a way for cultures to express themselves, but there are other ways to do this. Historians can learn a lot about ancient civilizations by studying their art. They can learn if the civilization had slaves, and they can learn how many gods they believed in.

Ancient Egypt had lots of different kinds of art, but most of it was intended to show that the pharaoh was seen as a god. The ancient Egyptians believed that the pharaoh was divine, and they used their art to communicate that idea. The earliest art was pictures called **reliefs**. Reliefs were carved into stone, but instead of carving the picture, the artist carved away everything except the picture. It makes the image stand out from the stone.

They also painted the inside of their tombs. The paintings show the deceased person enjoying the afterlife. The paintings also show some of the ordinary parts of ancient Egyptian life, like hunting and farming. This art has been preserved because it was shut up inside tombs for thousands of years. We can still see a lot of the original colors. As the people advanced their skills, the paintings became more and more detailed.

The ancient Egyptians also made **sculptures**. They usually made sculptures out of hard stone, and you can see many of their sculptures today. Ancient Egyptian sculptures face forward stiffly, and they show the real faces of people.

Ancient Egypt had lots of beautiful art, but it wasn't the only civilization creating art. Aksum also made a lot of art. We know it was different from ancient Egyptian art, but not as much of it survived. Aksum made pottery. It was usually decorated with **geometric patterns**. A geometric pattern is a shape that repeats itself many times. The most popular shape was the Christian cross, but other shapes were added to the pottery with stamps, decorative etching, and painting.

We don't have any statues from Aksum, but the bases that remain show its statues must have been impressive. Historians believe that one of the bases was intended to support a metal statue that was three times taller than a person. There are some smaller figurines of women and animals. Sadly, most of their art is now gone. Most of Aksum's tombs were looted. The little we have shows that Aksum made some impressive art during their time in ancient Africa.

Chapter 9 Activity Challenge

Can you identify which of these monuments are from ancient Africa?

The pyramids of Giza

The Colosseum

Stelae

Nubian pyramids

The Parthenon

Step Pyramid of Djoser at Saqqara

Stonehenge

The Great Sphinx

Chapter 10: Myths and Religion

Religion was a very important part of ancient Africa. The people had special religious practices. They also had myths about their gods, which helped them understand the world around them. In some ancient African civilizations, priests had a lot of power. They even had some power over the king! Each culture had its own religious practices, but there are some similarities between the different civilizations.

Ancient Egypt worshiped many different gods and goddesses. Some think that ancient Egypt had about two thousand different gods and goddesses. Can you imagine trying to remember all of those different deities? Each village had a specific god that they worshiped. **Horus** and **Osiris** were the most popular gods. Horus was the god of the sky. Osiris was the god of the afterlife.

The afterlife was very important to the ancient Egyptians. They believed that part of the soul called the **ka** remained in the body after death. The **ba** was the part that left the body at death. You need to have both the ka and the ba to still be you, so the Egyptians learned how to **mummify** bodies. They wanted to preserve the body to make sure that the person would have a good afterlife. Mummies were usually buried with jewels and food, which the Egyptians believed the soul would enjoy in the afterlife.

To get into the afterlife, you had to first go to the Hall of Truth. There, **Anubis** weighed your soul against an ostrich feather. Anubis was the god of the dead, but he was different from Osiris. If your soul was lighter than an ostrich feather, you got to go to the afterlife. If it was heavier, then it was eaten by **Ammit**, a demon with the head of a crocodile and the body of a lion. No one wanted to have their souls eaten, so the people tried to live good lives.

A picture of Ammit.
https://commons.wikimedia.org/wiki/File:Ammit_BD.jpg

The ancient Egyptians also believed the pharaoh was divine. When the pharaoh died, he or she would become a god. During their life, the pharaoh was the **mediator** (a person who communicates ideas between different groups of people) between the people and the gods. The priests helped with the temples and appeased the gods, but it was the pharaoh's responsibility to keep the gods happy.

Kush followed many of the same religious practices that ancient Egypt followed, especially early in its history. The people worshiped the same gods, and they took care to preserve people for the afterlife. They even built little pyramids as tombs. Between 350 BCE and 350 CE, some of the Kushites began to follow local gods. The most popular one was **Apedemak** (ah-pa-de-mak). He was the god of victory and good harvests.

Another traditional religion in Africa comes from the **Dogon** people (doh-gon). They still practice their traditional religion today in the country of **Mali** in West Africa. Their religion is mostly focused on the star Sirius, which they call **Po Tolo**.

The Dogon people have an important religious ceremony every sixty years. This event celebrates something that happened three thousand years ago. The Dogon people believe they were visited by beings from a planet near Sirius. The **Hogon** (ho-gun) is the main religious leader of each village. He dresses and acts to remind the people of the creation myth, which is very important to the Dogon culture.

Kanaga mask.

Many ancient religions were built on mythology. Here are a few myths from the civilizations we have looked at in this book.

Ancient Egyptian Creation

In the beginning, the universe was filled with darkness and chaos. There were no trees or people or even gods. Then, one day, a hill called the **Benben** appeared. The god **Atum** stood on the hill. He looked at the dark chaos and realized he was alone. That made Atum sad, so he created **Shu** and **Tefnut** (tef-nuht) by spitting. Shu and Tefnut then created the world by giving birth to two more **deities** (gods or goddesses). Their names were **Nut** and **Geb**. Nut was in charge of the sky, and Geb was in charge of the earth.

Nut and Geb were deeply in love, but the other gods didn't like it. Some versions of this myth say that Shu separated them, and some versions say Atum separated them. Either way, Nut was placed high in the sky. This separated Nut and Geb.

A typical depiction of Amun, another important Egyptian god.
He was the god of the sun and the air.

Nut eventually gave birth to five children. They were **Osiris**, **Isis**, **Set**, **Nephthys** (nef-this), and **Horus**. These were the five most popular gods in ancient Egypt. In the beginning, Osiris was made the king of Egypt. Humans were created by Atum's tears, and they lived on the earth that was formed by Nut and Geb.

How Osiris Became the Ancient Egyptian God of the Afterlife

Osiris was known as the god of the afterlife, but he didn't start out that way. At first, Osiris was the king of Egypt. He was a good king. Under his rule, Egypt was beautiful and peaceful. His brother **Set** was jealous. He wanted to be king and have all the power that Osiris had. So he made a plan. He made a chest that fit Osiris. Then, he lured Osiris into the chest, slammed the lid shut, and threw it in the Nile River.

Isis was very upset about it. Osiris was her brother and her husband, and she didn't want him to die. When Isis found Osiris's body, she began working on bringing him back to life.

Set found out, and he was very angry. He went to the place Isis had hidden Osiris's body. He cut it up into forty-two pieces and hid the pieces all around Egypt. Isis had to go find all the pieces. By the time she was done, she was still missing a piece. It had been eaten by a fish! Even though she was able to bring Osiris back, he couldn't be the king of Egypt anymore. Instead, he became the king of the afterlife.

Outside of Egypt

There are many different deities, spirits, tricksters, and heroes in African mythology. For example, some tribes in East Africa called their main god **Mulungu** (ma-lun-gu). Some tribes of West Africa called their main god **Amma** or **Olorun** (o-lor-un).

For a long time, African mythology was not written down. While many civilizations and tribes had written languages, they either did not write down their myths, or those documents were lost to history. Instead, many people in Africa had an **oral tradition**. That means they told their stories verbally instead of writing them down. There were even professional storytellers. It was their job to remember all the stories and tell them to the people.

Historians are working on writing down the myths that people in Africa still tell. The mythology of Africa is as varied as its civilizations. As you now know, those civilizations were very important to the development of the ancient world.

Chapter 10 Activity Challenge

Can you choose the correct answer for each question?

Dogon	Osiris	Mulungu	mummification
Amma	Apedemak	Atum	oral tradition

1. The god of the ancient Egyptian afterlife was called _____.

2. The Hogon was a religious leader for the _____ people.

3. Ancient Egyptians used _____ to preserve the body for the afterlife.

4. The main god was called _____ by some West African tribes.

5. Some East African tribes called their main god _____.

6. The first god in ancient Egyptian mythology was _____.

7. A popular Kushite god was _____.

8. Much of Africa practiced an _____ when it came to telling their myths.

If you want to learn more about tons of other exciting historical periods, check out our other books!

AFRICAN HISTORY FOR KIDS

A CAPTIVATING GUIDE TO THE HISTORY OF AFRICA

CAPTIVATING HISTORY

Bibliography

"Ancient Africa: Ancient Carthage." *Ducksters*. Accessed March 2022.
https://www.ducksters.com/history/africa/ancient_carthage.php

"Ancient Africa: Empire of Ancient Ghana." *Ducksters*. Accessed March 2022.
https://www.ducksters.com/history/africa/empire_of_ancient_ghana.php#:~:text=A
ncient%20Ghana%20ruled%20from%20around,lands%20as%20they%20saw%20fit

"Ancient Africa: Kingdom of Aksum (Axum)." *Ducksters*. Accessed March 2022.
https://www.ducksters.com/history/africa/kingdom_of_aksum_axum.php

"Ancient Africa: Kingdom of Kush (Nubia)." *Ducksters*. Accessed February 2022.
https://www.ducksters.com/history/africa/kingdom_of_kush.php

"Ancient Egypt." *Britannica Kids*. Encyclopedia Britannica. Accessed February 2022.
https://kids.britannica.com/kids/article/Ancient-Egypt/353087

"Ancient Egypt: Government." *Ducksters*. Accessed March 2022.
https://www.ducksters.com/history/ancient_egyptian_government.php

"Ancient Egypt: Old Kingdom." *Ducksters*. Accessed February 2022.
https://www.ducksters.com/history/ancient_egypt/old_kingdom.php

"Ancient Egypt: New Kingdom." *Ducksters*. Accessed February 2022.
https://www.ducksters.com/history/ancient_egypt/new_kingdom.php

"Ancient Egypt: Pyramids." *Ducksters*. Accessed February 2022.
https://www.ducksters.com/history/ancient_egyptian_pyramids.php

"Ancient Egypt: Timeline." *Ducksters*. Accessed February 2022.
https://www.ducksters.com/history/ancient_egyptian_timeline.php

"Ancient Egyptian Alphabet." *History for Kids*. Accessed March 2022.
https://www.historyforkids.net/ancient-egyptian-alphabet.html

"African Mythology." *Myths and Legends*. Accessed March 2022.
http://www.mythencyclopedia.com/A-Am/African-Mythology.html

"Berbers." *Britannica Kids*. Encyclopedia Britannica. Accessed March 2022.
https://kids.britannica.com/kids/article/Berbers/601928

"Biography: Hannibal Barca." *Ducksters*. Accessed March 2022.
https://www.ducksters.com/history/africa/hannibal.php

Britannica, T. Editors of Encyclopedia. "Africa." *Encyclopedia Britannica*. March 29
2018. https://www.britannica.com/place/Africa-Roman-territory

---. "Aksum." *Encyclopedia Britannica*. September 5, 2021.
https://www.britannica.com/place/Aksum-ancient-kingdom-Africa

---. "Dogon." *Encyclopedia Britannica*. April 13, 2018.
https://www.britannica.com/topic/Dogon

---. "Ghana." *Encyclopedia Britannica*. April 22, 2020.
https://www.britannica.com/place/Ghana-historical-West-African-empire

---. "Piye." *Encyclopedia Britannica*, January 30, 2015.
https://www.britannica.com/biography/Piye

Cartwright, Mark. "Kingdom of Axum." *World History Encyclopedia*. Last modified March 21, 2019. https://www.worldhistory.org/Kingdom_of_Axum

"Dogon." *Academic Kids Encyclopedia*. Accessed March 2022.
https://academickids.com/encyclopedia/index.php/Dogon

Donn, Lin. "Ancient African Kingdom of Ghana." *Mr. Donn's Site for Kids & Teachers*. Accessed March 2022. https://africa.mrdonn.org/ghana.html

---. "Ancient Egypt for Kids: The Three Kingdoms." *Mr. Donn's Site for Kids & Teachers*. Accessed February 2022. https://egypt.mrdonn.org/3kingdoms.html

---. "Ancient Egypt for Kids: The Two Lands and King Menes." *Mr. Donn's Site for Kids & Teachers*. Accessed February 2022. https://egypt.mrdonn.org/twolands.html

---. "Ancient Kingdom of Kush (Nubia)." *Mr. Donn's Site for Kids & Teachers*. Accessed February 2022. https://africa.mrdonn.org/kush.html

---. "Hannibal and the Punic Wars." *Mr. Donn's Site for Kids & Teachers*. Accessed March 2022. https://rome.mrdonn.org/hannibal.html

"Egyptian Architecture." *History for Kids*. Accessed March 2022.
https://www.historyforkids.net/ancient-egyptian-architecture.html

"Egyptian Art." *History for Kids*. Accessed March 2022.
https://www.historyforkids.net/ancient-egyptia-art.html

"Egyptian Daily Life." *History for Kids*. Accessed March 2022.
https://www.historyforkids.net/egyptian-daily-life.html

"Egyptian Pyramids." *History for Kids*. Accessed February 2022.
https://www.historyforkids.net/egyptian-pyramids.html

"Egyptian Religion." *History for Kids*. Accessed March 2022.
https://www.historyforkids.net/egyptian-religion.html

"Kingdom of Kerma: Facts for Kids." *Kiddle Encyclopedia*. November 2021.
https://kids.kiddle.co/Kingdom_of_Kerma

"Kush." Encyclopedia Britannica. Accessed February 2022.
https://kids.britannica.com/kids/article/Kush/353352

"Kushite Religion." Encyclopedia of Religion. *Encyclopedia.com*. February 28, 2022.

https://www.encyclopedia.com/environment/encyclopedias-almanacs-transcripts-and-maps/kushite-religion

Mark, Joshua J. "Ancient Egyptian Mythology." *World History Encyclopedia*. Last modified January 17, 2013. https://www.worldhistory.org/Egyptian_Mythology

---. "Carthage." *World History Encyclopedia*. Last modified May 29, 2020. https://www.worldhistory.org/carthage

---. "The Kingdom of Kush." *World History Encyclopedia*. Last modified February 26, 2018. https://www.worldhistory.org/Kush

---. "Menes." *World History Encyclopedia*. Last modified January 29, 2016. https://www.worldhistory.org/Menes

"New Kingdom." *History for Kids*. Accessed February 2022. https://www.historyforkids.net/new-kingdom.html

New World Encyclopedia Contributors. "Berber." *New World Encyclopedia*. Accessed March 2022. https://www.newworldencyclopedia.org/p/index.php?title=Berber&oldid=1063295

---. "Ghana Empire." New World Encyclopedia. Accessed March 2022. https://www.newworldencyclopedia.org/p/index.php?title=Ghana_Empire&oldid=1005238

"Old Kingdom." *History for Kids*. Accessed February 2022. https://www.historyforkids.net/old-kingdom.html

"Religion of Ancient Egypt: Facts of Kids." *Kiddle Encyclopedia*. Last modified July 16, 2021. https://kids.kiddle.co/Religion_of_Ancient_Egypt

"Roman Africa." *Oxford Reference*. Accessed March 2022. https://www.oxfordreference.com/view/10.1093/oi/authority.20110803095354714

Sue, Caryl. "The Kingdom of Kush." *National Geographic Society*. July 2018. https://www.nationalgeographic.org/media/kingdoms-kush

"The Archaic Period." *History for Kids*. Accessed February 2022. https://www.historyforkids.net/the-archaic-period.html

"The Great Sphinx." *History for Kids*. Accessed February 2022. https://www.historyforkids.net/the-great-sphinx.html

"The Kingdom of Kerma (2500-1500 BC)." *Think Africa*. November 2018. https://thinkafrica.net/the-kingdom-of-kerma-2500-1500-bc

Some Great Books to Check Out:

Gods and Goddesses of Ancient Egypt: Egyptian Mythology for Kids. Morgan E. Moroney. 2020.

Egyptian Diary: The Journal of Nakht. Richard Platt. 2014

Who Was King Tut? Roberta Edwards. 2006.

Made in the USA
Coppell, TX
27 November 2022

87220553R00050